THIS BOOK BELONGS TO

_____

_____

_____

To join our mailing list and see other titles available

Website: www.captaintimpublishing.com
Email: info@captaintimpublishing.com

Color it

the

Read it

the

Trace the word

the the the

Write the word

Write the word in a sentence

I go to ____ school.

Find and circle

the	they	see	we	
go	were	the	are	
it	are	you	is	the
went	the	their	was	

Connect the letters to spell the word

t s u r e

a m h z i

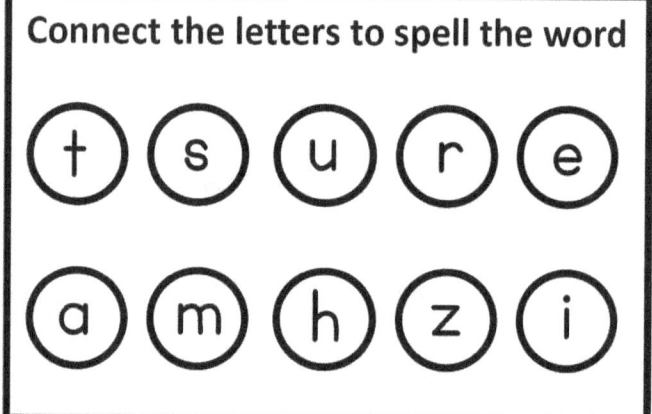

Color it

Read it

Trace the word

Write the word

Write the word in a sentence

plays football.

Find and circle

the	they	go	we
play	he	the	are
it	are	you	is	he
he	the	their	were

Connect the letters to spell the word

Color it

at

Read it

at

Trace the word

at   at   at

Write the word

Write the word in a sentence

The train arrives ☐ the station.

Find and circle

these	his	go	at
play	he	at	each
it	are	you	is	if
he	at	their	many

Connect the letters to spell the word

z a u g f

d m t x i

Color it

but

Read it

but

Trace the word

but   but   but

Write the word

Write the word in a sentence

I am hungry [   ] I have nothing to eat.

Find and circle

he	said	his	go	at
is	how	he	at	but
it	them	but	is	if
look	but	their	time

Connect the letters to spell the word

(b) (a) (t) (g) (y)

(d) (u) (l) (j) (i)

Color it

there

Read it

there

Trace the word

there   there

Write the word

Write the word in a sentence

I will go ☐ today.

Find and circle

there	his	now	at
how	there	at	but
it	them	but	into
use	but	their	part

Connect the letters to spell the word

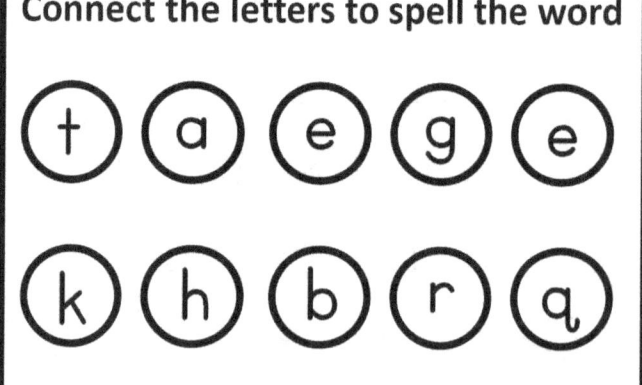

t   a   e   g   e

k   h   b   r   q

Color it

will

Read it

will

Trace the word

will   will   will

Write the word

Write the word in a sentence

I ⬜ go to school tomorrow.

Find and circle

he	will	his	now	go
how	there	at		we
are	it	out	but	will
day	but	will	part	

Connect the letters to spell the word

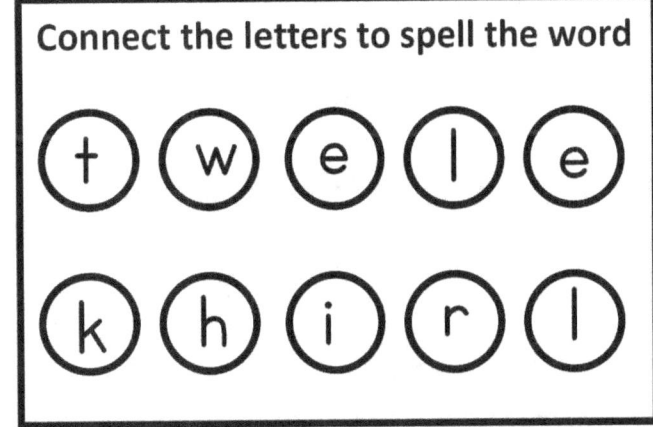

t w e l e

k h i r l

Color it

some

Read it

some

Trace the word

some   some

Write the word

Write the word in a sentence

I want to drink [ ] water.

Find and circle

he   will   his   some
from   there   or
are   as   some   but
who   as   will   some

Connect the letters to spell the word

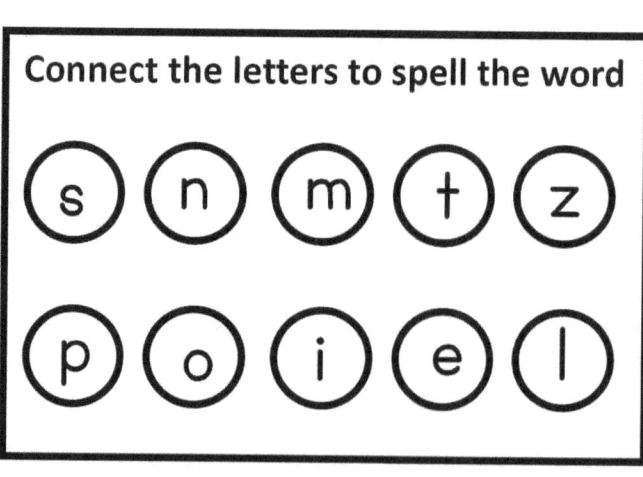

Color it

two

Read it

two

Trace the word

two two two

Write the word

Write the word in a sentence

I have [ ] brothers.

Find and circle

he two his write
from we two or
is as some two
one as two into

Connect the letters to spell the word

s n t x o
q f i w l

Color it

my

Read it

my

Trace the word

my my my

Write the word

Write the word in a sentence

I love ☐ family.

Find and circle

you this my write
from we my or
is are some can
my as with into

Connect the letters to spell the word

m j v x o
q y i w h

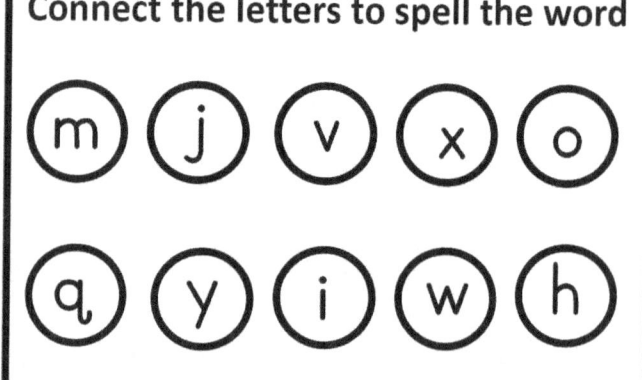

Color it

Read it

Trace the word

find   find

Write the word

Write the word in a sentence

He could not [   ] her.

Find and circle

you	this	my	find
find	we	my	at
is	are	some	can
my	as	find	will

Connect the letters to spell the word

Color it

Read it

of

Trace the word

of of of of

Write the word

Write the word in a sentence

I am not afraid ☐ dogs.

Find and circle

look this   my   find
find   we   of   am
is   of   some   can
his   as   find   of

Connect the letters to spell the word

k a o r z
w i f c i

Color it

Read it

Trace the word

was   was   was

Write the word

Write the word in a sentence

It ☐ cold yesterday.

Find and circle

part	this	my	was
find	we	of	am
are	of	was	can
was	as	may	of

Connect the letters to spell the word

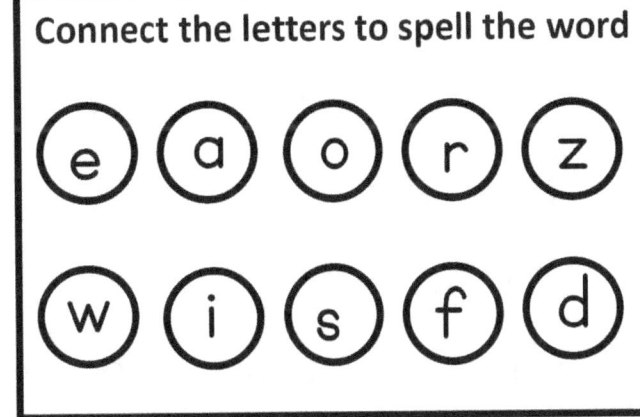

Color it

be

Read it

be

Trace the word

be   be   be

Write the word

Write the word in a sentence

I want to ☐ a doctor.

Find and circle

get this   be   was
time be   of   am
be   of   see   can
was   as   may   be

Connect the letters to spell the word

e   a   o   b   z

w   i   s   e   d

Color it

Read it

Trace the word

not   not   not

Write the word

Write the word in a sentence

She is [ ] your teacher.

Find and circle

get   many   or   was
time   be   of   not
not   of   with   can
that   as   not   be

Connect the letters to spell the word

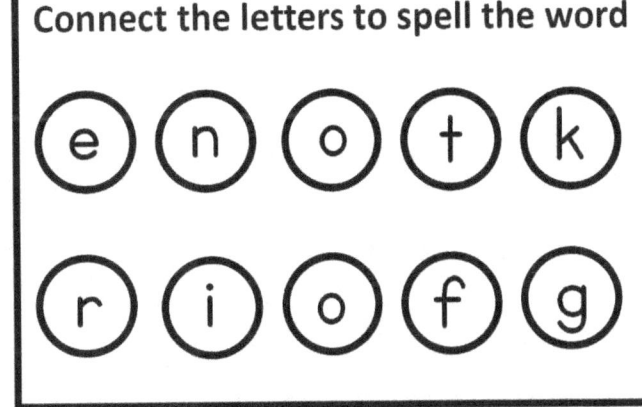

e   n   o   t   k

r   i   o   f   g

Color it

use

Read it

use

Trace the word

use　　use　　use

Write the word

Write the word in a sentence

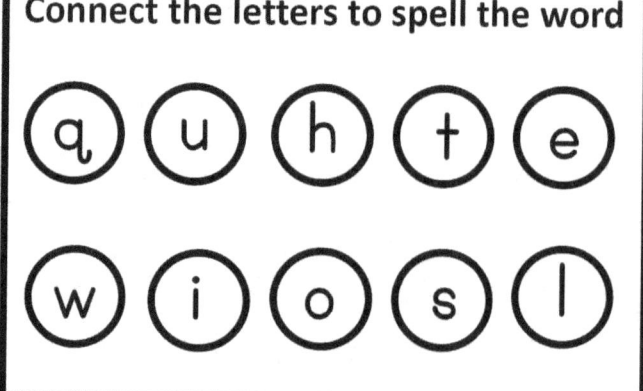

Do not ⬜ the scissors.

Find and circle

get　use　or　was
use　be　of　day
which　of　use　can
use　as　we　be

Connect the letters to spell the word

q　u　h　t　e
w　i　o　s　l

Color it

Read it

Trace the word

up   up   up

Write the word

Write the word in a sentence

Jack climbs ☐ the hill.

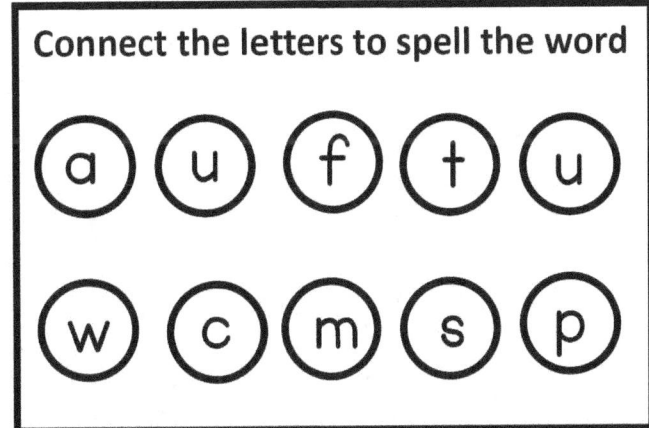

Find and circle

up	use	or	was
come	be	up	day
said	of	use	one
you	as	up	be

Connect the letters to spell the word

a   u   f   t   u

w   c   m   s   p

Color it

her

Trace the word

her   her   her

Write the word

Write the word in a sentence

She loves ⬜ sister.

Find and circle

see   do   or   her
come   her   up   day
they   of   use   her
you   her   up   get

Connect the letters to spell the word

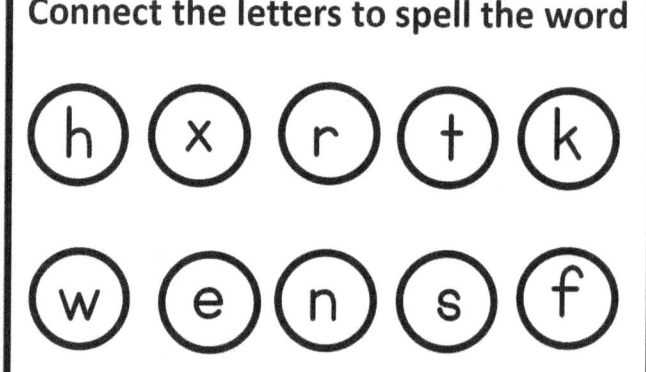

h   x   r   t   k

w   e   n   s   f

Color it

Read it

Trace the word

more more

Write the word

Write the word in a sentence

I need some ☐ time.

Find and circle

see do more him
more her up day
other of more her
been her up more

Connect the letters to spell the word

g o w e j
m t r s f

Color it

than

Trace the word

than   than

Write the word

Write the word in a sentence

I love cats more ☐ dogs.

Find and circle

each do   want   than
could than   up   day
other is   made   her
been her   up   than

Connect the letters to spell the word

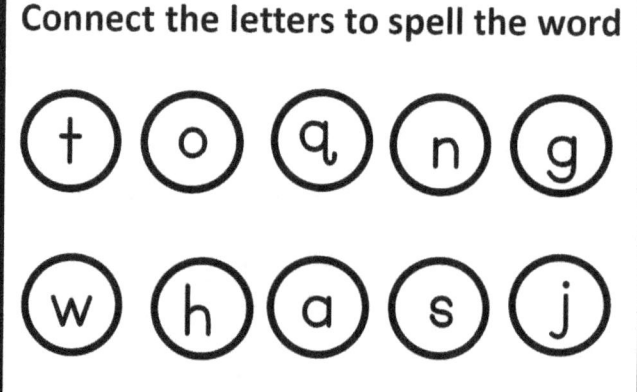

Color it

long

Read it

long

Trace the word

long long

Write the word

Write the word in a sentence

She has ______ hair.

Find and circle

each	do	long	than
long	than	up	get
from	is	long	can
look	her	up	long

Connect the letters to spell the word

l o q g s

m h n k j

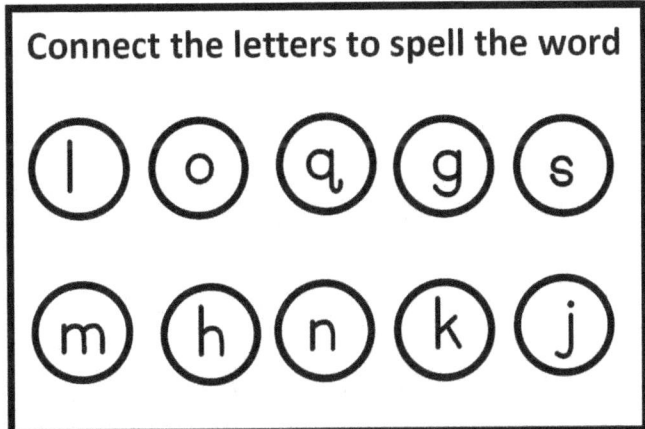

Color it

and

Read it

and

Trace the word

and   and   and

Write the word

Write the word in a sentence

I love my mum ⬜ dad.

Find and circle

called	we	long	him
long	and	up	get
now	is	and	can
made	her	up	and

Connect the letters to spell the word

f o a y s

v h n d j

Color it

for

Read it

for

Trace the word

for for for

Write the word

Write the word in a sentence

I want eggs ______ breakfast.

Find and circle

called	we	like	him
long	for	up	get
for	by	and	your
go	for	up	and

Connect the letters to spell the word

f o r y s

z g n c j

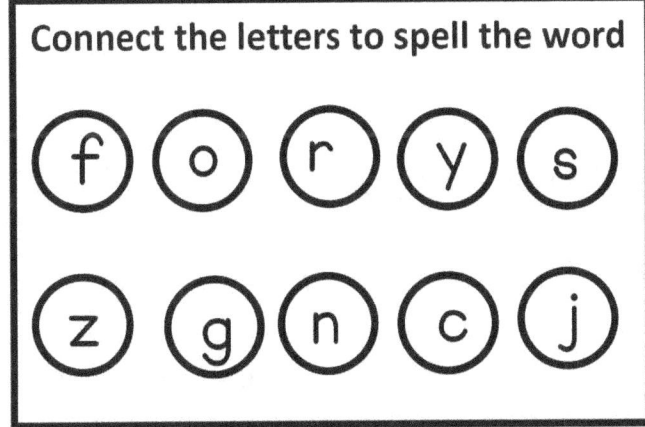

Color it

this

Read it

this

Trace the word

this this this

Write the word

Write the word in a sentence

I don't like ⬜ .

Find and circle

first	we	this	him
this	for	up	get
now	by	and	this
said	for	up	and

Connect the letters to spell the word

t p i y x

z h n s l

Color it

what

Read it

what

Trace the word

what   what

Write the word

Write the word in a sentence

I know [   ] your name is.

Find and circle

make	we	what	him
this	for	up	get
which	by	and	what
what	for	down	and

Connect the letters to spell the word

a w i y x

z h t s l

Color it

an

Read it

an

Trace the word

an   an   an

Write the word

Write the word in a sentence

I want to be ⬚ actor.

Find and circle

there   an   when   him
this   many   an   is
see   an   and   what
words   for   him   and

Connect the letters to spell the word

(g) (f) (a) (y) (w)

(z) (x) (n) (d) (l)

Color it

Read it

Trace the word

other   other

Write the word

Write the word in a sentence

I have ⬜ toys.

Find and circle

other   an   when   him
with   other   an   is
see   an   who   been
other   for   or   and

Connect the letters to spell the word

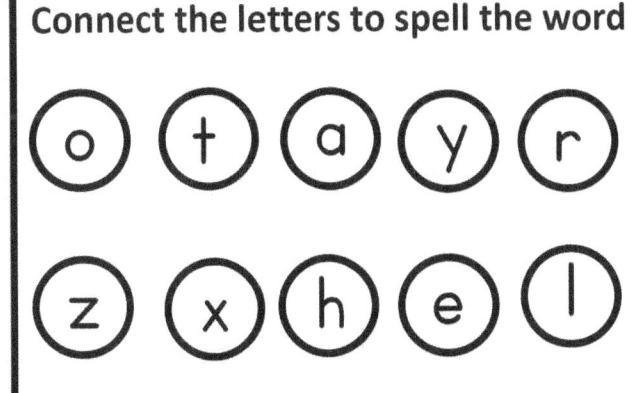

Color it

would

Read it

would

Trace the word

would   would

Write the word

Write the word in a sentence

I ☐ like some rice.

Find and circle

its   an   would   him
one   would   an   is
said   an   who   are
would   for   or   and

Connect the letters to spell the word

k   q   u   y   d
w   o   h   l   m

Color it

Read it

Trace the word

write   write

Write the word

Write the word in a sentence

I ⬜ in my book.

Find and circle

its   write   all   him
one   may   an   down
said   an   write   are
write   out   or   and

Connect the letters to spell the word

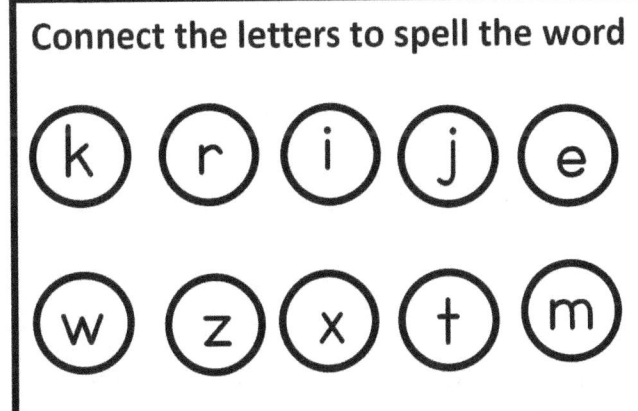

Color it

first

Read it

first

Trace the word

first   first

Write the word

Write the word in a sentence

My [   ] name is John.

Find and circle

its   first   all   him
one   first   an   not
been   an   were   are
has   out   first   and

Connect the letters to spell the word

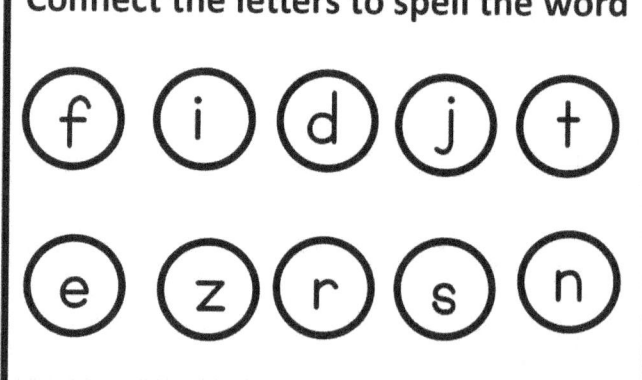

(f) (i) (d) (j) (t)
(e) (z) (r) (s) (n)

Color it

Read it

Trace the word

down   down

Write the word

Write the word in a sentence

She fell ☐ the stairs.

Find and circle

am down all him
one do fell not
had an were down
has out down and

Connect the letters to spell the word

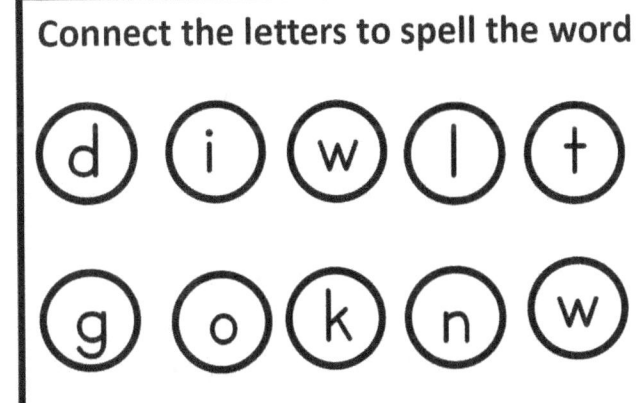

d i w l t

g o k n w

Color it

a

Read it

a

Trace the word

a a a a

Write the word

Write the word in a sentence

He is ☐ good boy.

Find and circle

now long all a
one a fell not
had a were down
but out a and

Connect the letters to spell the word

q a l k t
f e v s x

Color it

Trace the word

house   house

Write the word

Write the word in a sentence

My [   ] is very beautiful.

Find and circle

we   see   all   on
one   on   fell   house
house   a   were   down
go   house   on   and

Connect the letters to spell the word

Color it

have

Read it

have

Trace the word

have   have

Write the word

Write the word in a sentence

We ☐ a party tonight.

Find and circle

we   have   all   on
way   on   fell   not
had   a   have   come
have   word   on   and

Connect the letters to spell the word

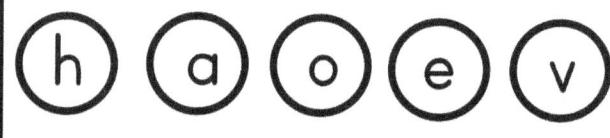

Color it

all

Read it

all

Trace the word

all all all

Write the word

Write the word in a sentence

I love ______ my friends.

Find and circle

we have all on
make on fell not
so a all come
all word on and

Connect the letters to spell the word

s a o k z
g e l l x

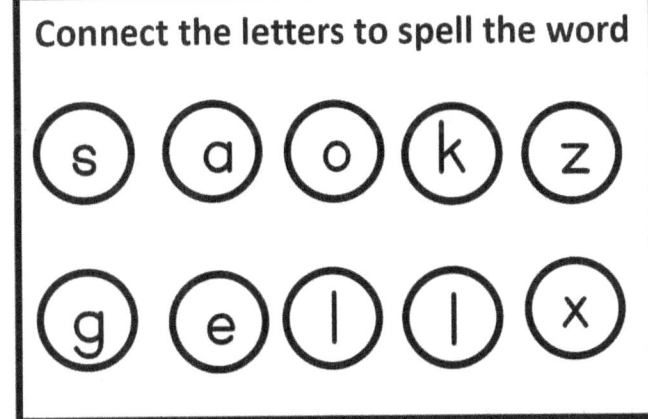

Color it

each

Read it

each

Trace the word

each   each

Write the word

Write the word in a sentence

They are helping ☐ other.

Find and circle

we each   all him

make on fell not

each an   all with

all people on each

Connect the letters to spell the word

e a n h z

g x c l t

Color it

about

Read it

about

Trace the word

about   about

Write the word

Write the word in a sentence

Tell me [   ] your hobbies.

Find and circle

we	about	all	now
make	it	fell	not
about	an	all	him
one	about	on	each

Connect the letters to spell the word

(l) (a) (g) (o) (u)

(y) (x) (b) (h) (t)

Color it

make

Read it

make

Trace the word

make   make

Write the word

Write the word in a sentence

I can [   ] a sand castle.

Find and circle

we if   all make
make it fell not
people so all many
one make on part

Connect the letters to spell the word

s a k o d
m x b e c

Color it

go

Read it

go

Trace the word

go   go   go

Write the word

Write the word in a sentence

I [ ] to school by bus.

Find and circle

two go all make
have it fell not
people her go come
go make on part

Connect the letters to spell the word

v a g f d
m x o k h

Color it

water

Read it

water

Trace the word

water   water

Write the word

Write the word in a sentence

I drink [＿＿＿] everyday.

Find and circle

were it   all water
have it   fell not
water her is come
go way on water

Connect the letters to spell the word

w   a   g   e   d

n   x   t   u   r

Color it

day

Read it

day

Trace the word

day day day

Write the word

Write the word in a sentence

It was a sunny ______ .

Find and circle

she it all day
day it fell not
made day is come
go you on these

Connect the letters to spell the word

d y z e d
a x t k r

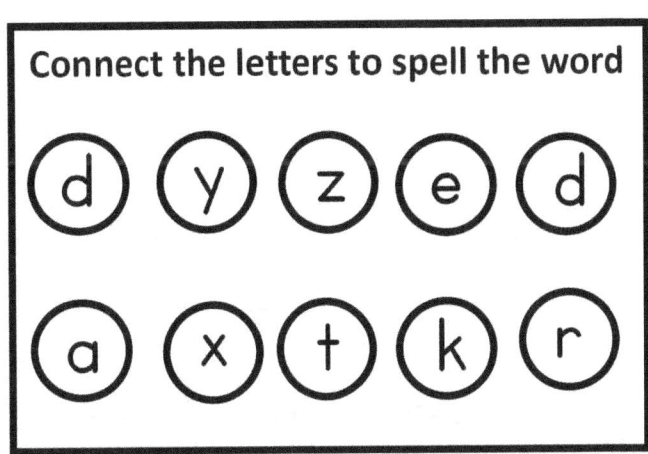

Color it

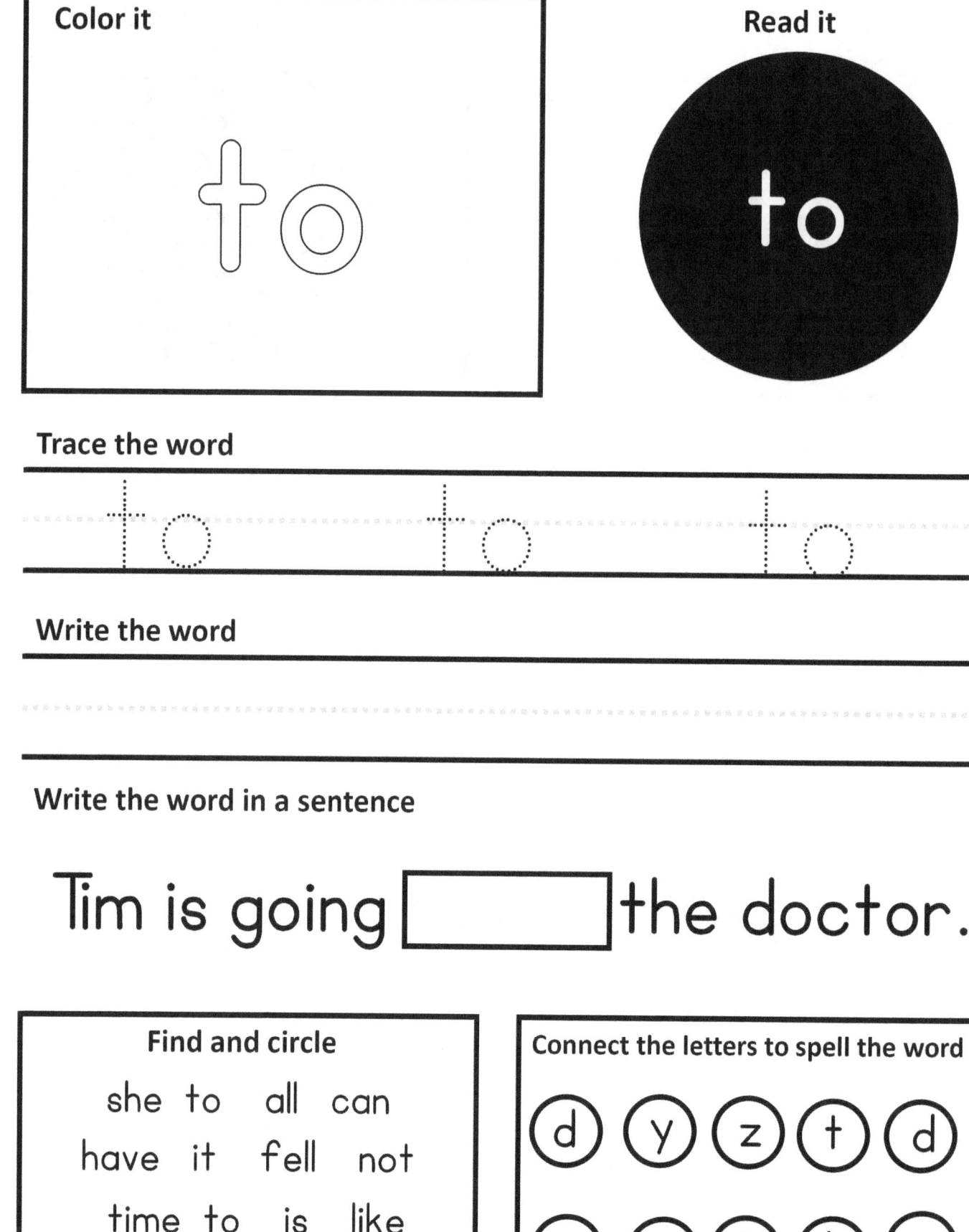

Read it

to

Trace the word

to   to   to

Write the word

Write the word in a sentence

Tim is going [ ] the doctor.

Find and circle

she   to   all   can
have   it   fell   not
time   to   is   like
to   you   on   these

Connect the letters to spell the word

d   y   z   t   d

a   x   t   k   o

Color it

are

Read it

are

Trace the word

are   are   are

Write the word

Write the word in a sentence

We [   ] very happy.

Find and circle

but   to   all   can

when   it   are   not

time   my   is   are

to   are   on   some

Connect the letters to spell the word

c   r   z   w   d

a   x   t   e   o

Color it

from

from

Trace the word

from   from

Write the word

Write the word in a sentence

My house is far [   ] school .

Find and circle

but to   see   from
from it   are   not
where my   is   are
to   them   on   from

Connect the letters to spell the word

(f) (r) (z) (m) (d)

(s) (x) (o) (e) (v)

Color it

Read it

Trace the word

were   were

Write the word

Write the word in a sentence

We [   ] at the park yesterday.

Find and circle

were	to	see	made
from	it	are	not
each	my	is	were
to	were	on	from

Connect the letters to spell the word

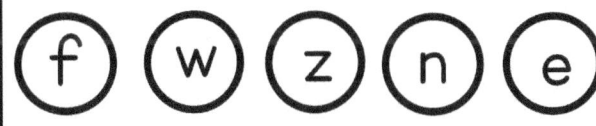

Color it

which

Read it

Trace the word

which   which

Write the word

Write the word in a sentence

[   ] color do you prefer?

Find and circle

its to   see   which
which to   are   not
each by   is   were
I   were   if   which

Connect the letters to spell the word

Color it

Read it

Trace the word

out   out   out

Write the word

Write the word in a sentence

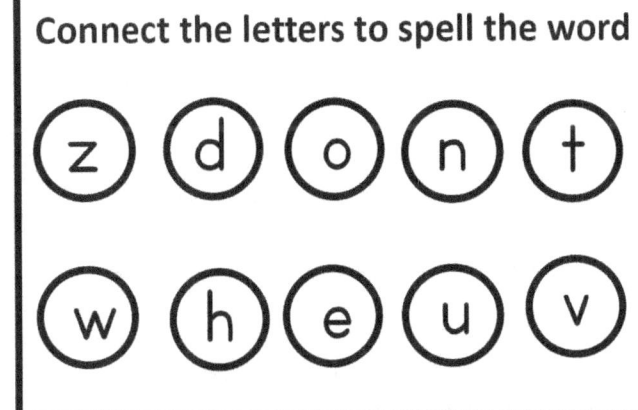

Find and circle

out	to	see	which
am	to	out	are
time	by	is	were
I	out	if	come

Connect the letters to spell the word

z d o n t

w h e u v

Color it

like

Read it

like

Trace the word

like   like   like

Write the word

Write the word in a sentence

I ⬚ eating chicken.

Find and circle

who	to	see	with
for	to	out	like
like	by	is	were
I	like	if	come

Connect the letters to spell the word

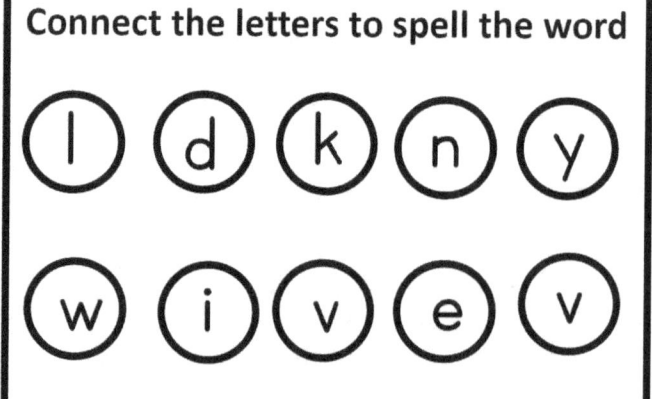

Color it

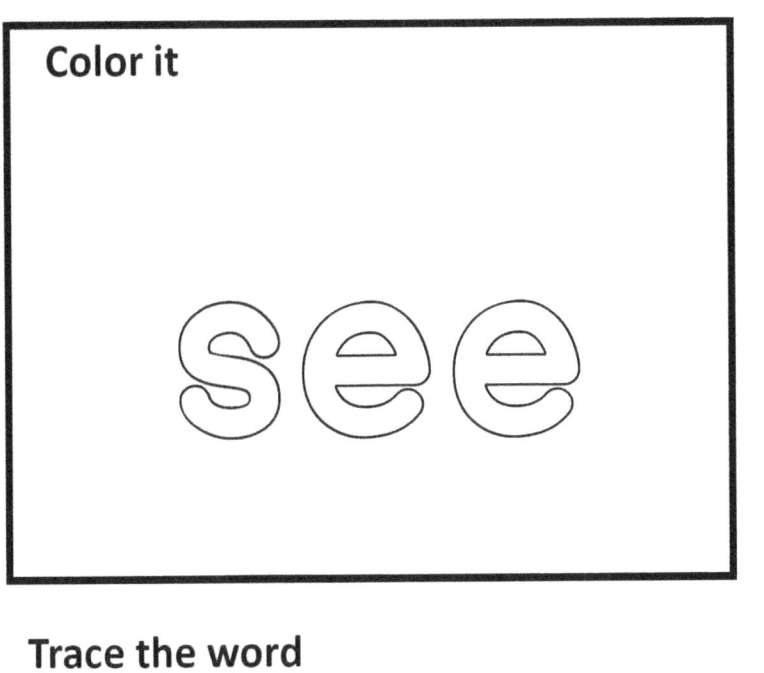

Read it

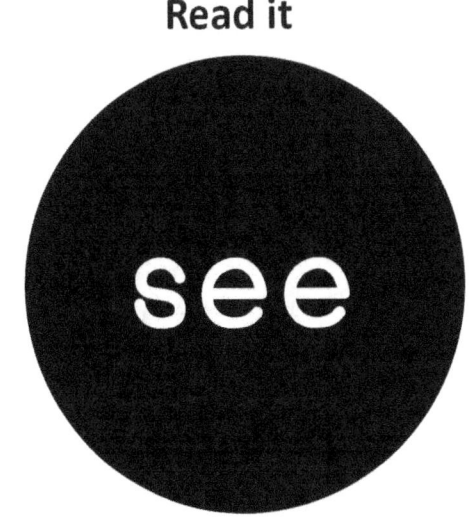

Trace the word

see   see   see

Write the word

Write the word in a sentence

I can ⬜ stars in the sky.

Find and circle

him	go	see	now
she	to	out	like
see	by	is	were
it	that	if	see

Connect the letters to spell the word

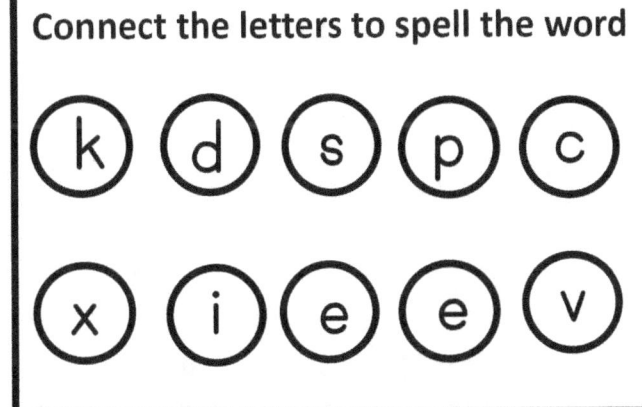

Color it

been

Read it

been

Trace the word

been   been

Write the word

Write the word in a sentence

It has ▢ raining all day.

Find and circle

him	go	as	many
she	to	out	been
been	by	is	she
it	been	if	way

Connect the letters to spell the word

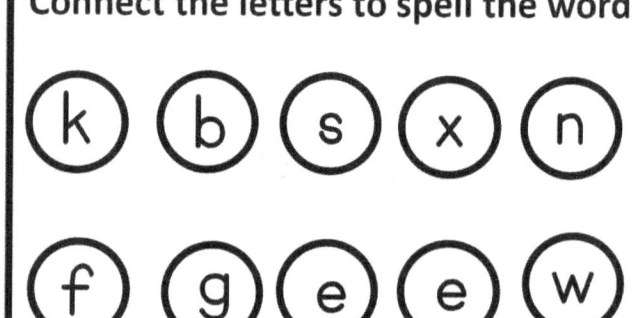

k   b   s   x   n

f   g   e   e   w

Color it

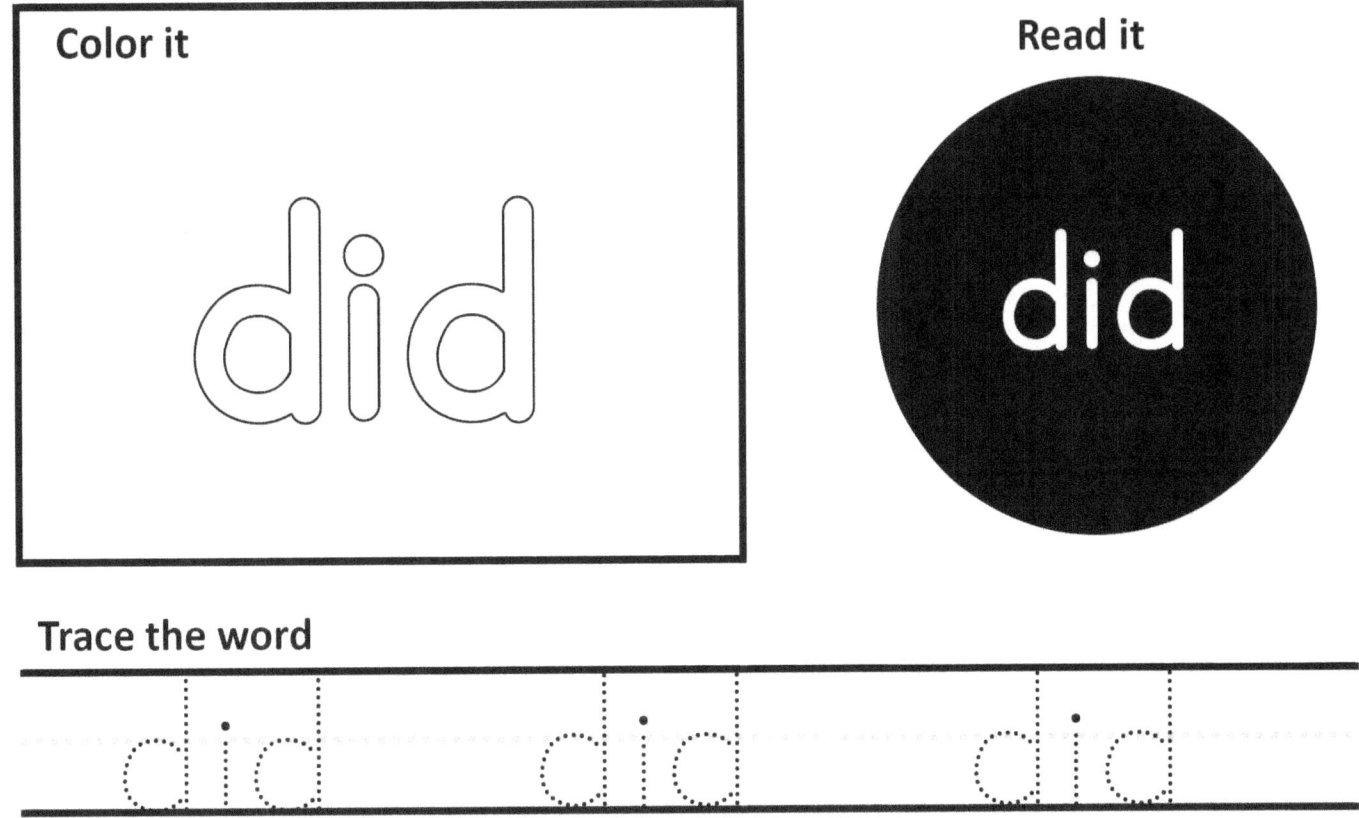

Read it

did

Trace the word

did   did   did

Write the word

Write the word in a sentence

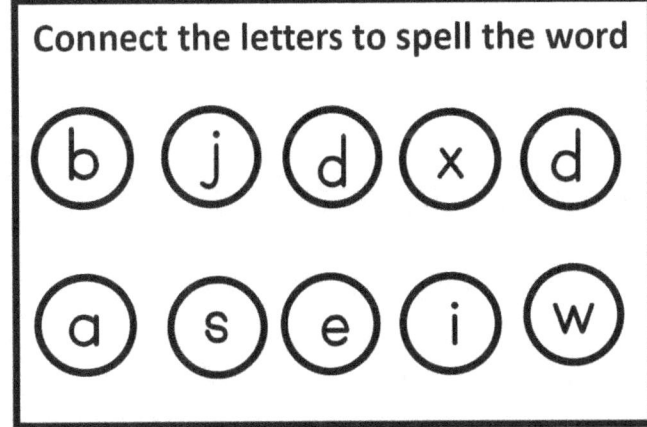

I ⬜ my homework.

Find and circle

did	go	out	your
she	to	did	with
make	by	is	did
you	did	if	way

Connect the letters to spell the word

b   j   d   x   d

a   s   e   i   w

Color it

in

Read it

in

Trace the word

in   in   in

Write the word

Write the word in a sentence

The cake is [____] the oven.

Find and circle

then go   out   come
she in   did   their
from by   in   did
how   in   if   made

Connect the letters to spell the word

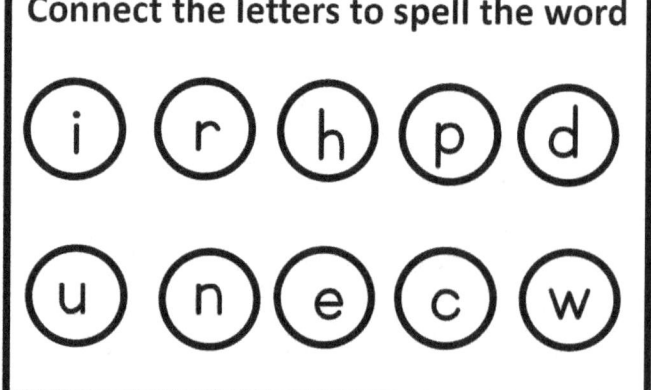

Color it

as

Read it

as

Trace the word

as   as   as

Write the word

Write the word in a sentence

You are the same age ⬚ me.

Find and circle

said no all come
she as did their
each by as did
have as if made

Connect the letters to spell the word

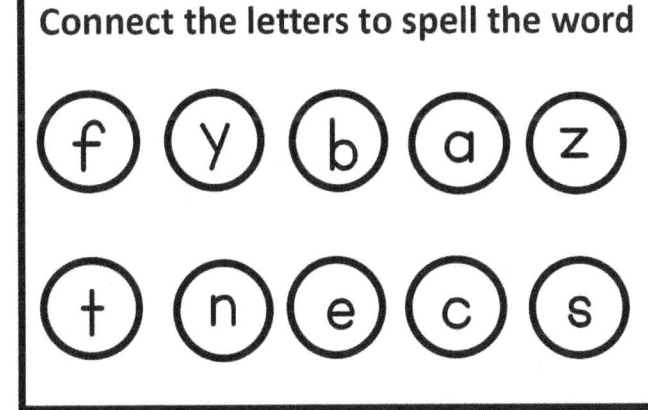

f y b a z

t n e c s

Color it

or

Read it

or

Trace the word

or   or   or

Write the word

Write the word in a sentence

Do you have any brothers ☐ sisters?

Find and circle

or   many   all   she
into   as   did   were
words   or   as   did
have   as   or   made

Connect the letters to spell the word

v   y   o   a   z

w   f   j   r   x

Color it

we

Read it

we

Trace the word

we   we   we

Write the word

Write the word in a sentence

It's time [ ] go to bed.

Find and circle

or we   all   them
you   as   did   were
look   or   we   did
have   we   or   then

Connect the letters to spell the word

b e o s q
w f d r x

Color it

she

Read it

she

Trace the word

she   she   she

Write the word

Write the word in a sentence

[   ] has beautiful hair.

Find and circle

its has   all   she
she as   did   were
could or   by   she
she his   or   other

Connect the letters to spell the word

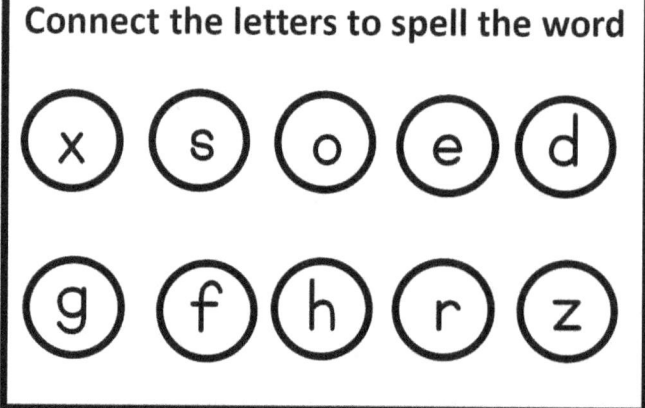

Color it

many

Read it

Trace the word

many   many

Write the word

Write the word in a sentence

I have ☐ cousins.

Find and circle

its many all which
from as did many
many or by she
your his or look

Connect the letters to spell the word

(m) (s) (n) (f) (m)

(z) (a) (c) (y) (z)

Color it

him

Read it

Trace the word

him   him   him

Write the word

Write the word in a sentence

I met ▢ yesterday.

Find and circle

its out   all   which
from   as   him   said
that   or   by   him
your   him   or   look

Connect the letters to spell the word

Color it

number

Read it

Trace the word

number   number

Write the word

Write the word in a sentence

Two is an even ⬚ .

Find and circle

its   out   all   number
number   as   him   said
that   or   by   water
see   him   or   may

Connect the letters to spell the word

Color it

called

Read it

called

Trace the word

called   called

Write the word

Write the word in a sentence

Grandma [ ] yesterday.

Find and circle

its go   all   called
words as   him   said
called or   if   water
see   him   or   called

Connect the letters to spell the word

c a m l e

v d l b d

Color it

get

Read it

get

Trace the word

get   get   get

Write the word

Write the word in a sentence

I [ ] up at 6:30 AM.

Find and circle

get   can   all   that
into   as   get   look
their   or   if   from
about   get   or   more

Connect the letters to spell the word

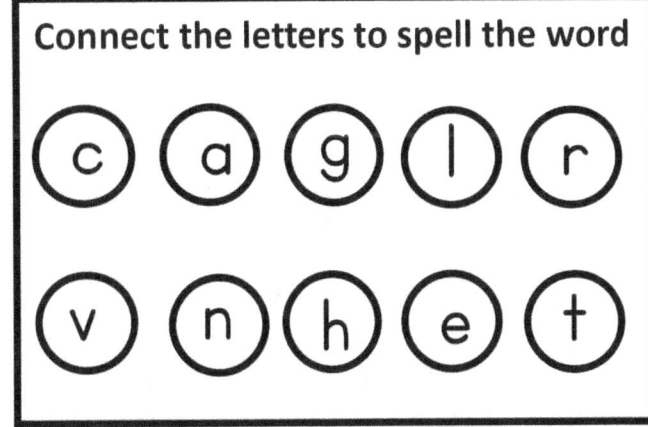
c   a   g   l   r
v   n   h   e   t

Color it

is

Read it

is

Trace the word

is   is   is

Write the word

Write the word in a sentence

My mum ⬜ great.

Find and circle

did   is   all   more
into   is   get   look
their   or   is   first
what   get   or   more

Connect the letters to spell the word

c   i   w   l   z

v   s   h   k   t

Color it

with

Read it

with

Trace the word

with with

Write the word

Write the word in a sentence

I am going to the zoo ______ Tom.

Find and circle

with is all like

into is had with

their or is first

with made or more

Connect the letters to spell the word

o w t l z

p i h k b

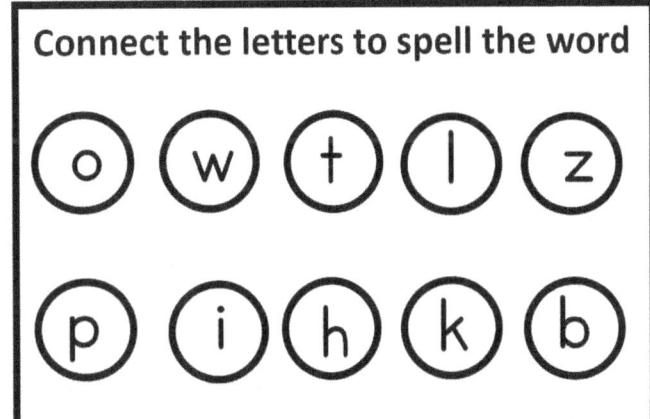

Color it

one

one

Trace the word

one   one   one

Write the word

Write the word in a sentence

I have ☐ brother.

Find and circle

one not all like
into is had one
their or be first
with one by more

Connect the letters to spell the word

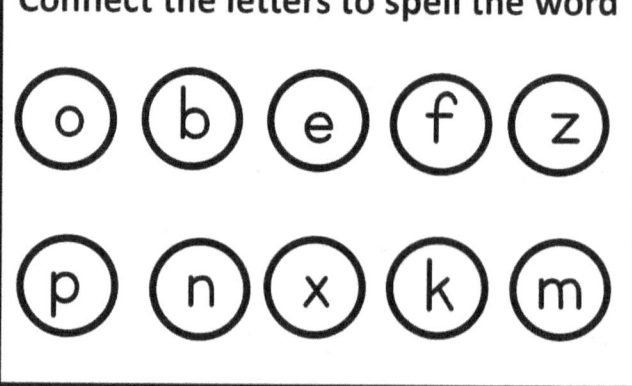

Color it

Trace the word

when   when

Write the word

Write the word in a sentence

do you wake up ?

Find and circle

see   not   get   like

into   as   when   one

their   do   be   when

when   one   by   more

Connect the letters to spell the word

Color it

do

Read it

do

Trace the word

do   do   do

Write the word

Write the word in a sentence

I will [   ] my best.

Find and circle

more	not	do	like
like	as	when	one
their	do	be	when
make	one	do	more

Connect the letters to spell the word

f   d   y   e   q

r   o   h   p   n

Color it

Trace the word

then   then

Write the word

Write the word in a sentence

What will happen ⬜ ?

Find and circle

then   am   do   like
but   for   then   one
their   do   be   then
part   one   of   more

Connect the letters to spell the word

t   c   y   e   r

v   o   h   p   n

Color it

into

Read it

into

Trace the word

into into into

Write the word

Write the word in a sentence

Peter dived [ ] the water.

Find and circle

would am do like
but this into may
could do be into
into one of more

Connect the letters to spell the word

d i y t w
v r n p o

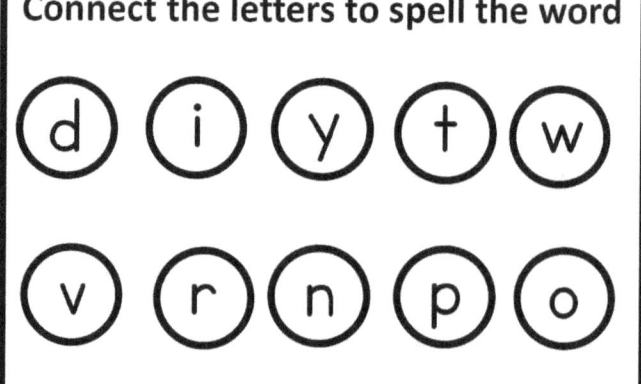

Color it

no

Read it

no

Trace the word

no no no

Write the word

Write the word in a sentence

I have ☐ sisters.

Find and circle

would am if no
no these into may
could do no into
day one no more

Connect the letters to spell the word

z i y n w
v r b u o

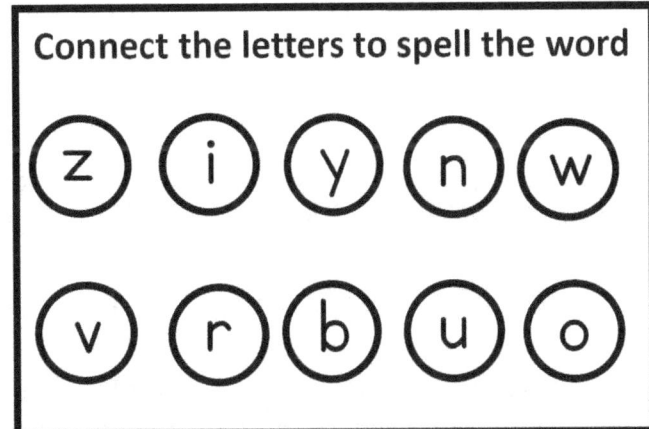

Color it

who

Read it

who

Trace the word

who   who   who

Write the word

Write the word in a sentence

☐ is your favorite teacher?

Find and circle

who   am   if   up
no   time   into   may
could   who   is   into
down   one   it   who

Connect the letters to spell the word

e   i   h   n   f

v   w   b   t   o

Color it

come

Read it

come

Trace the word

come   come

Write the word

Write the word in a sentence

Jane will [　　　] later.

Find and circle

with   come   if   way
no   time   into   may
come   her   is   into
down   one   it   come

Connect the letters to spell the word

(c)   (p)   (m)   (n)   (u)

(s)   (o)   (b)   (e)   (o)

Color it

you

Read it

you

Trace the word

you   you   you

Write the word

Write the word in a sentence

I miss [   ] .

Find and circle

find you   if   way
no   each   into   on
come   you   is   into
were   one   it   you

Connect the letters to spell the word

(a) (g) (v) (y) (u)

(s) (b) (c) (e) (o)

Color it

his

Read it

his

Trace the word

his his his

Write the word

Write the word in a sentence

He sat at ______ desk.

Find and circle

his you an way
no his into a
which you is his
said one it my

Connect the letters to spell the word

h i v w u
q b s e n

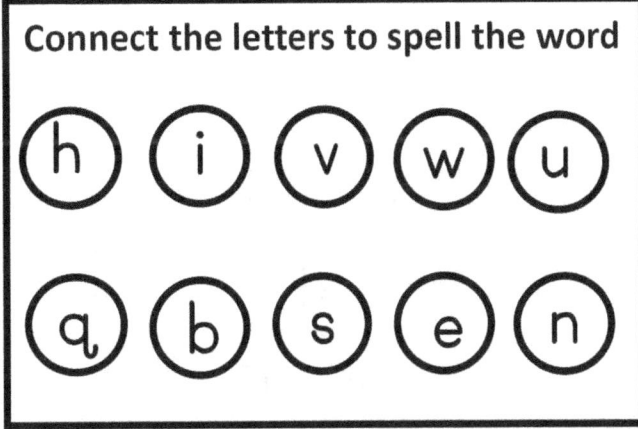

Color it

had

Read it

had

Trace the word

had   had   had

Write the word

Write the word in a sentence

We [   ] a lovely meal.

Find and circle

had two   an   way
up   his   into   a
what had   is   his
said one   it   had

Connect the letters to spell the word

(h) (x) (d) (w) (o)

(e) (a) (s) (e) (n)

Color it

your

Read it

Trace the word

your   your   your

Write the word

Write the word in a sentence

Wash [ ] face.

Find and circle

were	two	an	your
up	his	the	I
are	had	is	your
your	one	it	had

Connect the letters to spell the word

Color it

how

Read it

Trace the word

how how how

Write the word

Write the word in a sentence

[   ] old are you ?

Find and circle

how up an your
up there in its
are how is have
how am it had

Connect the letters to spell the word

h d w x c

k a o e r

Color it

them

Read it

them

Trace the word

them   them

Write the word

Write the word in a sentence

I want to see [_____] again.

Find and circle

were   up   we   them
up   there   in   of
are   them   is   have
you   an   it   them

Connect the letters to spell the word

f   d   e   x   z

t   h   v   m   r

Color it

time

Read it

Trace the word

time   time

Write the word

Write the word in a sentence

Have a good [   ] .

Find and circle

other   up   we   time
up   time   in   of
are   time   is   have
find   an   it   time

Connect the letters to spell the word

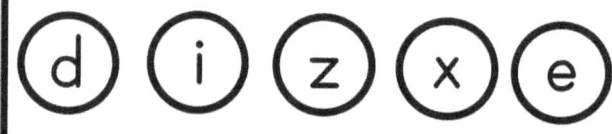

Color it

Trace the word

way   way   way

Write the word

Write the word in a sentence

Tom is on his ⬜ home.

Find and circle

down	up	we	way
up	way	in	if
are	time	is	way
not	way	it	time

Connect the letters to spell the word

z   i   w   x   y

t   h   f   a   p

Color it

am

am

Trace the word

am   am   am

Write the word

Write the word in a sentence

I [   ] pretty.

Find and circle

made up   am   this
up   and   am   out
am   time   is   way
can   am   it   make

Connect the letters to spell the word

h   g   w   k   m

t   h   f   a   p

Color it

made

Read it

made

Trace the word

made made

Write the word

Write the word in a sentence

I ______ a mistake.

Find and circle

made	its	or	this
in	made	am	use
am	look	is	made
up	made	it	were

Connect the letters to spell the word

h a c k d

m f d e p

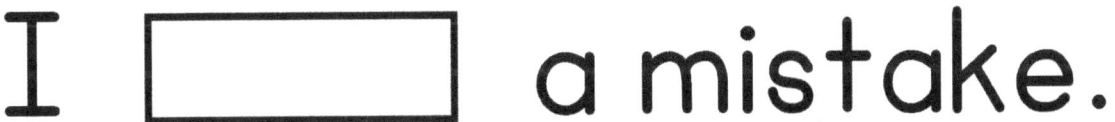

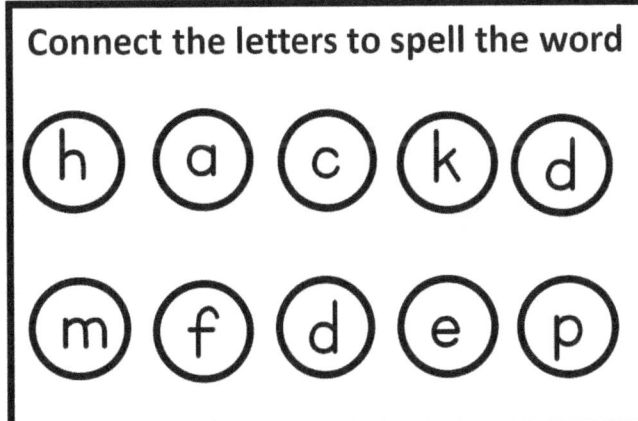

Color it

that

Read it

that

Trace the word

that that that

Write the word

Write the word in a sentence

Look at ▢ dog.

Find and circle

that   we   or   this
be   made   am   that
am   that   of   at
to   long   do   that

Connect the letters to spell the word

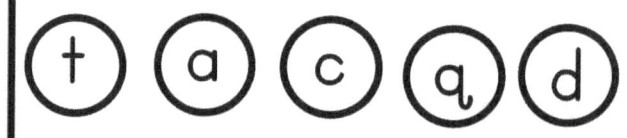
t   a   c   q   d

m   h   t   k   p

Color it

Read it

Trace the word

Write the word

Write the word in a sentence

☐ are my parents.

Find and circle

first we or they
be they am come
am like of they
to they do that

Connect the letters to spell the word

t a e q l

r h o y p

Color it

by

Read it

by

Trace the word

by   by   by

Write the word

Write the word in a sentence

He came ⬜ car.

Find and circle

called   we   by   they
by   they   in   made
if   like   by   they
by   they   do   people

Connect the letters to spell the word

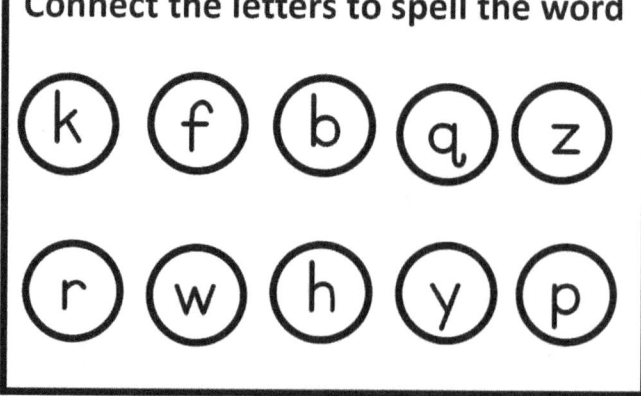

Color it

can

Read it

can

Trace the word

can   can   can

Write the word

Write the word in a sentence

She [   ] sing very well.

Find and circle

can we   by   my
by can in make
if see by can
by they can water

Connect the letters to spell the word

c f n q d

j a z y p

Color it

their

Read it

Trace the word

their their their

Write the word

Write the word in a sentence

I need ⬜ help.

Find and circle

their we by my
by can in their
if their by can
by their can have

Connect the letters to spell the word

Color it

Read it

Trace the word

these these

Write the word

Write the word in a sentence

[ ] are my books.

Find and circle

these we   as   use
by may   in   these
   if who   is   all
but they can   these

Connect the letters to spell the word

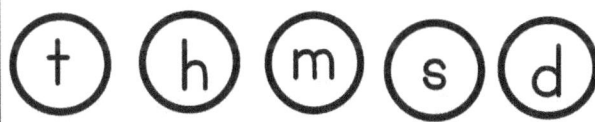
t h m s d

g a e y e

Color it

has

Read it

has

Trace the word

has   has   has

Write the word

Write the word in a sentence

He ☐ a pet cat.

Find and circle

has	we	for	use
by	has	in	these
if	who	two	can
but	has	now	these

Connect the letters to spell the word

r   h   n   s   d

b   a   e   y   p

Color it

could

Read it

could

Trace the word

could   could

Write the word

Write the word in a sentence

I wish I ☐ swim.

Find and circle

could we   for   did
by   have   in   could
he   up   could   can
is   has   now   could

Connect the letters to spell the word

r   o   n   s   d

c   a   u   l   p

Color it

night

Read it

night

Trace the word

night   night   night

Write the word

Write the word in a sentence

He stayed up late last ⬜ .

Find and circle

will   we   its   night
by   night   its   out
night   its   find   can
are   has   its   and

Connect the letters to spell the word

n   o   g   s   t

r   i   u   h   z

Color it

Read it

Trace the word

may   may   may

Write the word

Write the word in a sentence

It ⬚ rain.

Find and circle

may	we	if	for
up	was	all	may
he	its	may	can
see	may	no	and

Connect the letters to spell the word

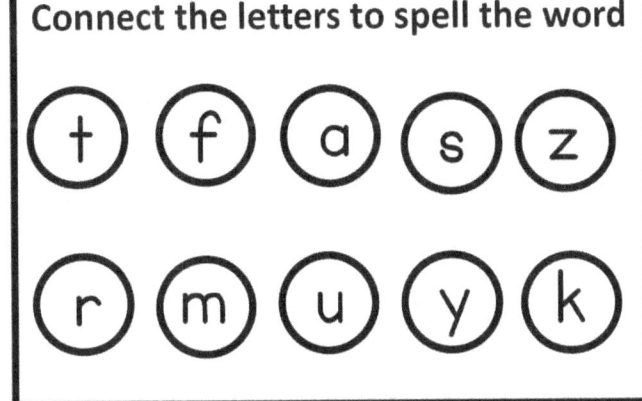

Color it

Read it

it

it

Trace the word

it   it   it

Write the word

Write the word in a sentence

is amazing.

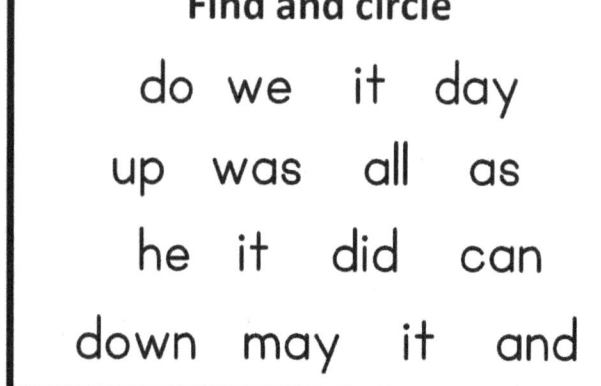

Find and circle

do we it day

up was all as

he it did can

down may it and

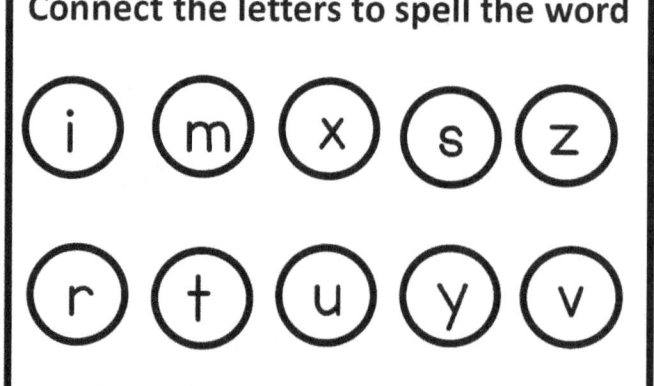

Connect the letters to spell the word

i m x s z

r t u y v

Color it

Read it

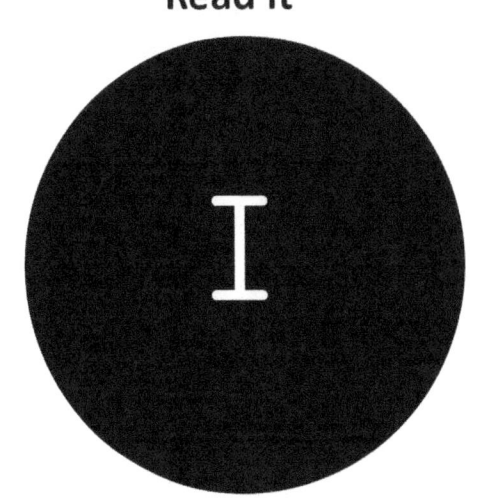

Trace the word

Write the word

Write the word in a sentence

[   ] am a dentist.

Find and circle

some we   I   day

I   were   all   him

he   I   did   get

they   may   I   and

Connect the letters to spell the word

(I) (m) (d) (x) (z)

(r) (h) (u) (y) (v)

Color it

words

Trace the word

words   words

Write the word

Write the word in a sentence

My book has many ⬚ .

Find and circle

words look   I   see
is   were   for   him
he   words   did   up
they   words   on   and

Connect the letters to spell the word

w   m   r   x   s

n   o   u   d   v

Color it

said

Read it

said

Trace the word

said   said   said

Write the word

Write the word in a sentence

She [   ] goodbye.

Find and circle

said look   she   we

is said   for   no

him words   said   up

were said   on   may

Connect the letters to spell the word

z a r x p

s o i d v

Color it

if

Read it

if

Trace the word

if   if   if

Write the word

Write the word in a sentence

We will get wet ⬚ it rains.

Find and circle

day	that	she	if
if	will	for	no
him	if	said	up
these	when	if	may

Connect the letters to spell the word

s a r f g

l m i d v

Color it

so

Read it

so

Trace the word

so so so

Write the word

Write the word in a sentence

I am ____ happy.

Find and circle

way	that	so	he
if	will	for	so
him	so	said	use
time	out	so	may

Connect the letters to spell the word

s a r m y

t n o d v

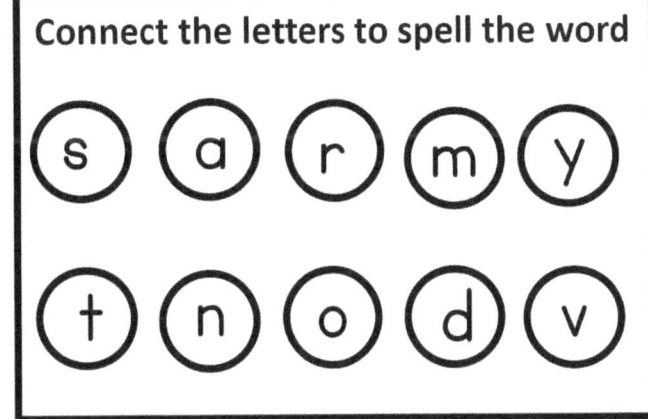

Color it

look

Read it

look

Trace the word

look   look   look

Write the word

Write the word in a sentence

You [   ] very nice.

Find and circle

look that   so   his
in   will look for
look so   said use
more out   on part

Connect the letters to spell the word

x   a   r   o   y

f   l   o   d   k

Color it

Read it

Trace the word

people   people

Write the word

Write the word in a sentence

Be kind to old ⬚ .

Find and circle

people that   so   his
in   will   people   am
look   is   people   use
down   out   it   part

Connect the letters to spell the word

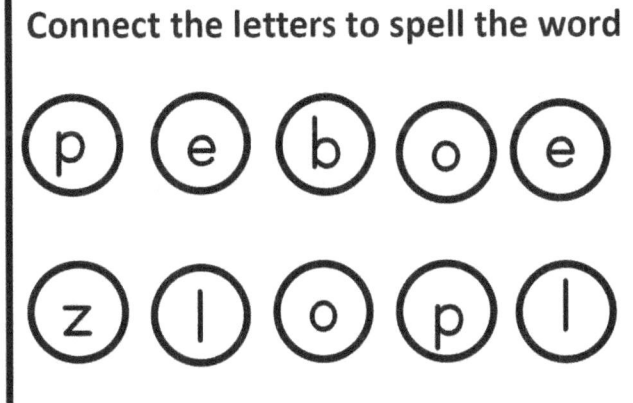

Color it

now

Trace the word

now   now   now

Write the word

Write the word in a sentence

She is studying [　　　] .

Find and circle

now   that   up   can
in   will   now   am
their   is   people   has
now   out   its   part

Connect the letters to spell the word

Color it

Read it

Trace the word

want   want

Write the word

Write the word in a sentence

I [   ] to go to the zoo.

Find and circle

want long up she
in will part am
see go like want
been out its want

Connect the letters to spell the word

Color it

ride

Read it

ride

Trace the word

ride   ride   ride

Write the word

Write the word in a sentence

Jane wants to [   ] her bicycle.

Find and circle

want long up ride
in ride part am
see ride like want
been out its want

Connect the letters to spell the word

r s d t b
w i n e i